The Glass Half Full

Samuel Isaias Lora

PublishAmerica
Baltimore

First printing

ISBN: 1-4241-9858-5
PUBLISHED BY PUBLISHAMERICA, LLLP
www.publishamerica.com
Baltimore

Printed in the United States of America

Querido Bebo,
No hay forma de agredecerte
por tu ayuda con este libro
Espero hacer muchas memorias
contigo para poder escribirlas!

Thank you for your support.
Wishing you the best
of luck. con Amor.
Samuelito

Dedication

I dedicate this book to the wonderful forces that have kept me going, aiming for a better self. Even though it would take me years to realize or to verbalize, you help me grow daily. Your love, your care, your support and your unbelievable persistence on getting to know me and love me for me. I owe the 'better self' to you.

From now forward, the road lays simply ahead. It's easier to see since we have been trapped by life's irony. Our relationship will flourish. Don't fear.

I love you with all of my heart and is now my duty, along with yours, to work on this amazing relationship.

Te quiero mucho Papa.

Thank You(s)

To the core that holds me still
In a home that is rare in existence
Support—Stability—Love
Words don't describe nor define
The shoulders to cry on
The hands to hold my stance
The words to cure my aches
The protection of my fragile heart
I thank you Mom & Dad
Sister, brother and best bud

When I used my PJ's as protection
Until Love found me
To the Journey of it's direction
From Brasilia to Paris
With Love as its destination
I thank you

The force that educates and loves me
For whom I aspire to be
Can't imagine life without such affection
Love you "grammy"

Because distance never cracked our affinity
You make me feel protected
To you I owe much...Madrina

Mental stimulation with psychology
Musical intermission by the alphabet
The A-toms
The Greek Gods
The T-wins

I thank you

Heartbreakers
Mind players
Bed chasers
And Love makers
To hurt me is to make me blunt
To scare me is to build me up
To lie expect share and intimidate
I thank you
I'm stronger from the moment I began

To the end of my beginnings
The knight guard of the dark skies
To the force which defines my life
The force defining love
Thank you for experiences
For this wonderful opportunity
I dedicate my words my life my Love
To you. To all.
Samuel

A WINNER

In Love since you showed me the way

With Love since you've given me in abundance

Out of Love since I have fallen off the tracks

In life since Love has been in its presence

Alone standing waiting to be heard

In your arms safe from the wonders of the world

With your words transmitting through my lips

All along since Love is all I need and Love is all I receive.

The ONE

They think that you are useless but they don't know where
you stand

Insignificantly mentioned
Secret purposes nobody needs to know
But as I love contradiction
I will let the secret flow
You are who you are -and-
You are in my heart because you fulfill every need it has
The one to complete
The one that indeed
Has turned my life right upside-down
The one, needless to say, is mentioned in every sentence of my
days
No actual need to specify your stance
Since you claim it with such beauty
You are the ONE for me that is all I need to mention

They think that you are useless because they don't know who
you are.

Sink Myself in Words

Heard of such bliss
A voice to keep within
Is it possible to achieve
Losing self-control?

Heard of such talk
But can't believe so
Defining myself alone
No more
And riding of control
Letting another take the stride

Bliss indeed
But where to find
I sink myself in words
To find the right defined

I sink myself in love
To find myself alive

I believe
In losing self control
I believe that someday
Somebody I will love

The Ways of a Hand

Know it's horrible to say
but want somebody for when changes come
My Way
About to embark on an unknown climax
and there is no one to hold
My Hand
Never thought of being this fragile
Can't help but wonder why
This exhilaration will cease in a few
In Time
Just a break in routine
that will come and patch
My Feelings
back in time

Your Hand in My Hands

Tracing the dots on my skin
with the light in your eyes
The moment is scarce
abundant with time
Lonely can mean
whatever I want
But in my life is
a dream gone awry
I open my eyes
the picture will fade
No longer to hold
your love through my hands

You Say Honesty, I Say Potato

"You're telling me what I want to hear," I told him as he
sighed.
Then, he cocked his head as if a response was emanating from
my mouth.
After realizing so would not be, he moved his body.
Erect.
And closely whispered in my ear...
"I don't know what you want to hear."
Honesty was the last thing on my mind-
since I have heard those words before.
But content to hear what my ears can't live without.
Pretense comes close to heart.
"You've done this before. I can see by how you smirk.
But no worries, you'll be figured out sooner or later."
After the roof of my mouth was done with its vibrations,
I sat dumfounded at God's creation.
I smiled nonchalantly.
Proud taking my time.
The fear of an old one-
or a new one had left my mind.
I then thought of the curse.
Always coming back.
I shot that window of thought, and enjoyed the purity.
He had been laughing for some time when my trance was
finalized.
He then proceeded to kiss me on the lips.
I couldn't smell, I couldn't taste.
But he touched a funny nerve.
I never thought life's guarantees would meet me at my door.
"I like you. Or I could get to,"
he said excitedly.
He said honesty. I said tomato.

Cruising

Stepping out
The night is young
Not so as am I

Age is nothing but a digit
Which I'm hoping to receive
To call To keep

Eyes ever so wondering
Feet ever so willing
To search To find

One two three four five
The more the merrier
If one is trashed others to balance

Empty lights in my room
Lonely shoes by the bed
Two pillows to fill

Willing to steal
Steal a body
A thrill

Love is undefined
Not savored by my tongue
In life I cannot find
A truth but a cruising tone

Pin Up Boy

Certain ideas of what it could be
Of what it could feel like

The fulfillment of a first one
Soul mates are said to be like pin ups
Only an idea
Only a dream

I dream to be a pin up boy
To someone
Anyone
I'm sure it's indescribable
To cause that joy
That sense of stability
Maybe just an empty ideal

But can't stop thinking when it happens
When I become a whole person

When my smile
Like dominoes
Creates abundance of the same
When my touch
Like a release
Becomes the betterment of a bad day

I become a pin up boy
Only in my head
I dream away…

Outsider

I walked slowly within my pace
I walked as if lonely; by myself
Then I felt so warm inside
The feeling of empty just left my mind...I watched.

The two of them were in a trance
He stared into him like nobody else
His eyes half open amid the passion
Beyond carnality, he kept his stance
He groped a hand coming across his shoulder
And stopped the music coming from his lips
He closed his eyes and leaned forward
The moment, the seal of the perfect kiss.

Love Bus

Jump right in
Let's trust the driver
The destination
Eager and willing to understand
Must know how to deal
Not an easy task
The road is bumpy
But we can hold hands
Just keep your hands inside the vehicle
It will be an unexpected ride
Prepare to understand
Keep away with your hands
Not an easy task
In this Love Bus for life

Love is in the air

Johnnie brought a smile with him

He was kind enough to share it with me

I don't know if it was the timing or his charity

But love is in the air

Verbal Transition

Sometimes in the tone of a voice
In the taste of that voice you find joy
Even when disguised you find happiness
Momentary bliss from that voice

The power in your head knows no limitations
So with creating the words are sweet if not meant

To love on one's own is bad enough
Belief takes part and hope helps transition
Too many candidates never enough
To spread the angel wings and help that transition

From loneliness to hopes
From expectations to knowledge
Once we are spoken to boundaries fail
Sometimes a tone can build your world

Magic

You are going to be a problem
I can see it in your eyes
I know you want to jump into conclusions
I can see it in your smile
The perfect frame
Statuesque at greeting
Complementing mine
I'd love to see that
Elves running spreading joy and laughter
There's a mist of thickness
Roaming through fields of gold
Are you mine for the taking?

Love Letter

Coyly handed me a bridge
A connection
Such a gift in my hands

I met you for dinner
But my world was expanded
Expanded with your letter
By your heart

There was still leftover doubt
Yet your face was more beautiful
Than one of your modeling shots
You lost your vibrant ways
Succumbed to redness of the cheeks
And bowing of the head

Envelope was opened
Releasing its context onto the ground
On my world
Words poured onto my fingertips
Allowing me to touch you
Feel you
You care and I could sense it
With the weight of your words
Diction

Like a nonchalant love letter
Hiding behind a pretext of congratulations
Genuine interest
Now emblazoned in my poetry.

to NY

crowded shadows empty lights
plenty of meaning not lacking the sparks
stars magic more than bargained for
there is a sea of colors
waiting to be thrilled by my body
a tint of red stands out
a distinct shape disappears at such sight
no more expectations
purpose of this happy place
energy floating in pairs
roaming the colors the hasty space
minds collide emotions understood
crowded space but plenty of room
multi cultural experience
humor excelling limits
to go out is to wonder
to embark on new ground
the new world
want that to be the rest of my life
would you be the city that never sleeps for me
would you make me go t o n y

Guard

The times I see you
I wonder why I am no longer pressed over you
But somehow feel that we might work out
It's just something I think about

There's certain hope exuding from you
There's a certain love appearing on you

Your eyes say a lot
Though you try to step off
Try to be repulsed
You know that the trick doesn't work
Give into the love

I don't understand your troubles
But relate to your questions
Forgot about your meaningless excuses
Since they leave me bland
Since you try to hard
Then you let down your guard
You show me who you are
You show me hope you show me love

When you walk away
I don't rush like I used to
When you say there's no way
I don't frown like before
Now when you look into my eyes
I see love

Forgot about your excuses since they leave me bland
They leave me cold you try too hard
Let down your guard who you are
Give me hope show me love

A Way to You

You've done well with controlling my emotions
Every time I see your face I try my hardest
But end up loving you

I pretend not to but when I do
Your looks blow me away
Some stares you own
Because I see inside
Somewhere
You care and my hopes are endless
That's why I keep you there
In the back of my mind

I keep trying to make some sense
Yet something is stopping you
So I say okay
Then I forget until you walk to me
Giving me all the hope over again
Trying my hardest
But I end up loving you
Saying your name
I end up loving you

Many times I put an excuse to the situation
But being with you there's no explanation
There seems to be a way to you
Leaving me driving away with hope
There seems to be a way to you
So I end up loving you

I pretend not to but when I do
That way I keep you there

Excuses feelings and stares
Seeing your face saying your name
There seems to be a way
So I love you

Let's Dance All Night

Digits groping my waist
Heavy breaths on my neck
There's a body attached to mine
The music plays

Dancing is second nature
Loving is a new emotion
Being touched is a new tendency
Being wanted is a never-ending victory

Hold me close
Don't let me spin too fast
My mind is speeding with the beats
My mouth no longer holding the lyrics

Hold me tight
Grab my hand in yours
Attached by extremities
Hip to hip heart to heart

Digits groping my waist
Passion through your lips to my neck
Hold me close hold me tight
Take my hand
Let's dance all night

First Week of Love

I missed you today
Can't wait for your time card to be punctured
I need you more than your customers
Please come see me

Soon
We'll be together again
Hours on end can be unbearable
Too many can be too much

Come on hurry
Let's spend some time
Being quiet and translucent
Sit back and relax

Let's sit in your car
Pretend we have something to say
Hold my hand
Kiss my neck
Feel my heart
Through my shirt

I beat faster because of you
I wake to see you
I aspire to love you
I aspire to be yours

Can't wait to see you soon
I'll be waiting for you

HEAVEN (INSIDE)

The first break from your lips
Since I became entangled in your web
I sit here and miss your kiss
My stomach is worried and my breath doesn't set
Stability is hard to find
-I start to think-
Want to cry because you make me feel so good
(INSIDE)
Never thought that it could
Here I am in heaven
So emotional
-My heart is given to you-
Never felt like this before
The soundtrack of my ears doesn't help my state
But I feel so good
(INSIDE)
As if distance and time had trapped me
Cry for your departure
I am a wreck -because-
This time I can't control myself
I am in your hands
You make me feel so childish
The butterflies are killing me
Long to hold you
Hope this lasts and that the feeling is reciprocal
Now understand love songs
I stand alone in a multitude
Thinking about you- about love
These insecure thoughts
Ridiculous in my head
I'm in bliss- still near you
In my mind

Heart
Soul
My heart is opening and I can't take it
Back
In your hands
The beautiful feelings you create inside
Thinking of you I opt to cry
(Smile INSIDE)

The King of Bliss

Part passionate kisser
Part hopeless romantic
As long as you amuse me
Could try sarcasm since I am the King
Could try to figure out how I've fallen in Bliss
Yet this time I am no longer with me
The butterflies do help
Just writing to write
Just thinking to love
No longer alone
Bliss written on stone
Just writing to write
Just writing to show
I've fallen for you
Not falling alone

-Urging on a High-

I'm listening to the disc you gave me
The songs pile up
While I'm listening I fight the urge
Urge to disbelieve that someone loves me
You make me smile from where you are
I am not going to let my head get in the way
Anymore
I love you so
I urge for your touch but in the sweetest of ways
I love what you do to me
Hoping this will never change
Only grow with time
You make my heart smile
And my soul elevate to the skies

CLOSER

Hold me gently. You do.
Kiss me softly—
passion oozing through the skin.
That too.
You can carry me and
You can hug me close and
You can show me love.
I will let you do it all to me.
I'll give you me in order to achieve such completeness.

I cannot believe you winked at me!
What came over you? How would you know?
Of all my weaknesses;
You know me all too well.
I guess once is all you needed to read my transparent
attributes.
I am now glued to those wondering lips. To kiss. To keep.
You held my hand as you walked me outside
politely letting me achieve my dream
of being raunchy in a lift
as we lowered our inhibitions.
I thank you for the ride of my life.
Without crossing any lines.
Something hard to find.

Saying the right words at the right time
always with the best of sense.
Not worrying about overexposing yourself to me.
Not being less nor more than me.
You play me so beautifully.
Keeping track of all of my strings, of my sensibility.
Sensitivity, all too well recognized.

Spastic, here and there, you follow me.
There, and anywhere.
Thanks for understanding who we are dealing with.
A balance hard to keep.

Such view never dies in the back of my mind.
Such feelings never leave my lonely side.
Why am I so comfortable and not at all intimidated by such
strong four walls?
A new box to try to get accustomed with, but you make all
with an easement.
An easement of breaking into and breaking out of old habits;
Old tactics that you seem to be okay with.
You can dance with me when music is lacking its vibrations.
In a balcony, we have made a long-lasting memory.
As I took my shoes off and placed my feet on your couch, right
next to yours I realized.
I realized the unwritten agreement on your face was much too
present.
I will encourage my heart to fall deep into yours.
With you is that I ought to be.

I pray to God at night
and I thank him for the reasons why
you came back into my life
and brought such light to guide my heart.
Closer, you and me.
Closer we agree.
To live what's left to live with no insecurities.
I thank the angels for holding me tight
and to you for being there, just at the right time.

Kid with a New Toy

I guess you could call it jealousy
but it's not that I'm greedy; I just want your company.
I wish we would have everything we could.
I want to be in public and always be able to
show you off so people can see
that's why you are the one that makes me happy.
I guess I am acting like a kid with a new toy
but if you've got it, why not flaunt it?
Isn't that the way it has to be?
Sometimes I do look outside this magic box.
I linger in the darkness to find what I'm looking for.
I have in you all that I can
so I make sure I know where to run before you break my
heart.
It might be erroneous since the jinx is on the table
but the love is too strong
for me to know it's not a fable.
I linger in my imagination
to see if happiness can come from a creation; something in my
head for only me to know.
I wish I were wrong so I don't lose this love
but at times I think lessons take over what I know.
I cry, I smile, I have nowhere to go.
I pain, I gain but you is all I know.

I Wish I Knew

Incessantly praying that we are not in it to hurt
But what is there to do?
Living is all that's left
The twitch quickly expressed in your eyes
In your brows
As a new face would appear
Holding my hand through a sea of temptation
Bending backward for my love
Those are strong reasons
Reasons to want to love you
Increasingly fearful of the power of a single emotion
An emotion so strong to make me want you
Posses you
Being able to drive away with you
When all you do is pave the way
Teach me show me
Maturity
Nonchalantly impressed by my words and not phased by
surroundings
I innocently taming gained a space within your world
A world I want to dive into
There has to be a reason
Why to love you or closure
But my mind has only one task to figure out
Why it's so hard to keep track
To understand
Why loving you comes so easily
Those are emblazoned reasons I wish I knew
Reasons to know how to quit you

Lower note

Stance
Within perfection
A glance
Of contradiction
The eloquence of needs will succumb one in the end
Desire of the longing will only make your heart race
Want
Need
Crave to lower your tone
Come on you know you want to
Please play me a lower note

Timed Chance

Keep wantin' to trace your arch with the tip of my tongue
Why are you so tantalizing
I must be hours behind
Understand, I can't understand
How I've keep myself from making you mine
What if the blues all disappeared and all colours could blend
Making a gray-full of life within my grasp
If so could happen and no curse was made to be broken
And your eyes truly looked into my soul
We would be able to become one
For the rest of our lives...
Keep wantin' to be able to grasp each inch of your skin
And let the animal out of me
Able- you've made me
To feel the urge
To feel your power over me

If dreams came true
If the skies are blue- watching right above me
If my love is pure- you'll be mine in minutes

Thrill

Feeling the blood speed through my veins.
Each heartbeat beating faster than before.
Finally, leaving the arms to the side and letting the mind do
the walking.
Grasping for air through no brakes.
Keeping the eyes in a trance, with no way of turning away.
Finally, letting the heart do the talking.
I must know of this thrill.
Being in my immediate future.
Am I writing fate with these fins from hell?
No. No, no. I don't sell souls for a living.
And mine is intact. Thank you for caring.
There is no foul play, ask the judges for a verdict.
Just trying to maximize my aftermath.
Yes, yes, I understand. I am too wordy for your like.
But read between my lines, how many times have I repeated
myself?
Fine, I'll let it pass. I'll explain my feelings on another time.
But you must know that this is the end.
You cannot go back and apply the rule there.
This thrill is mine to keep, since you stole the last chance.
I know more than two beings is a party in the park.
One date is all I ask. This weekend is all I have. To keep up with
your tab.
But am I really playing when the push comes to shove?
Beyond it all, all I can think, is this thrill will be my savior.

The Scream

Walking across the bridge
Holding onto the rails
Looking into the distance
There is no end to what the view can tell
Alone only a shadow behind
Such presence will be the guiding light
So why is fear so culminating in the deepest of ways
Only feel like holding head with eyes wide shut
Such light such shadow only makes the one pray
Pray for love to be what kills the rest
Above it shines with orange and red
The shallow underneath creates a way to digress
Is tough to be on here to be the one to turn away
But the love is the light to make your heart hold its place

Reasons Behind

It's wrong

It's so wrong

I wish I wouldn't

I hope I'm not

Sometimes I think there might be something else

Something easier

But I know obstacles make it all better

As if for value

and leaving wouldn't count

But isn't staying for more facility?

I mean

there is fear in fleeing

So what can a person do to escape the fear of fearing?

Staying or leaving both conclude with cowardliness

I guess it's all in the reasons behind it

-Reason-

At first glance it was obvious
You had me at hello
Easement to your movements
A grace to your eyes
Distinctive way to stare
To wink this way to play the field
To mark the X
Territorial you were
Advantageous to your mission
Since you had me in a glance
For eternity
You were the proof of it all
Yet a curse to my heart

No More Blues

But want them within me
No more blues to contain myself
Still remember when
We met we shared the most memorable time
At first glance you captured my heart
My mind useless in your presence
In the presence of the blues

Many try to mimic your value
But they wind up falling apart
Cheap tricks is all they have
Up their sleeves nonetheless
You on the other hand
Held my interest from the start
Remembering the feeling of accomplishment
Of finding a soul mate at first try

The blues have been with me
Ever since you *drift away*
Stare after glow after glare after lust
You have created a lineup

You held my hand
And kissed me gently
The curse to my dreams
Goes ever so silently...

More Aggressive

I whispered sweet nothings in your ear
I convinced myself of my worth to you
But such action was not reciprocal
You advised me to be more aggressive toward what I want
You got what you wanted
You were left with a sore heart

A sore mind, your eyes can tell the story themselves
I still think about you, and yes a bastard I was
Through the years I tried to hide the facts
The fact that I played with your mind
You words sunk into my skull
'Cuz I was aggressive toward what I wanted
I wanted love I wanted you
I had you in my palm
Then let you go when you were had

I apologize, since you were my first
the guinea pig
Yet I still have you in my mind
At times feel as if you were the one to stay
Not in this case, since fate wrote you off
But what if actions spoke louder than words
Would you and I be driving into the sunset?

I wonder why and if and but
But there is no time to think behind
I should have not listened to you
I should not do as you said to do
You are there and I am here
And all I did was why I am here
I listened to you and you are not near
I'm aggressive toward what I want, but what is your quality?

Quality

Giving
There is proof to all you did
Your eyes, oh so effervescent
You know, the blues have got it made
There is no turning when you come this way
Light, after love, after lust
The presence of you is unmatched
Sometimes, the reason why individuals fall off the earth
No comparisons, to you, they are gone
Why must you be the opposite?
Why must you show the way to love?
There is no other ruler to measure with
No guarantees of being fulfilled
Your words, your ticks, your words, your kiss
You showed me a way, and I've been lost ever since

The first time I had seen your face the second time
Your face,
rapidly brighter away from me.
You have found all the things to fill up your heart.
- There was no more room for me.
You could live for the next hundred years without me around
- Without me holding your hands; you'd still be as fulfilled as
if I were.
It pains me nonchalantly, since I am in over my head, by
myself
within these four walls we built. On my own still- little hope
still.
The first time I had seen your face after our time apart
was when I realized that you no longer care as much
as much as my heart stills holds on.

Fact

It is funny how my heart is broken
But I still love you with each little piece.
At this point, after all we have been trough
You become a disappointment.
Hope was all I had for you, us, for I.
At this point, I don't think you care a bit.
Not a bit of what we had.
Blame me all you want, I still love you more than you ever
loved me.
And that's a fact.

Facts, I don't believe. This, you made of me.
Derailed my personality...

I have cried for you since I don't see where your feelings were
ever kept.
Your face still as ever will have to fade since thinking of you
makes me sob like a child.
I don't want.

No hand to hold, since mistakenly, I put all my eggs in your
basket.
Mistake, and right I wasn't.

I Was Wrong

I did not realize how badly my eyes wanted to speak
Tears are all they have on their lips
Abundance has never been so absolute
My cheeks are smooth within the humidity

Drop, drop, drop, drops drop

My emptiness resonates
Echoing through my insides
This love was not strong enough

I hate it!

You were right
They were right
I prevailed
And I was wrong

Left Alone

It's after midnight the day has been silenced
As I take one breath I can hear my solitude
The television is on in the background assuming its task
Liberating my eyes from focusing on the problem
I have been left alone
The ice cream I'm eating doesn't fill any void
But it tingles my tongue as if trying to
Another ad plays

call to find love

A website to find someone to adore
But I did and was left alone
That's the thing

I was there

No need to call I had found the one
Then I let it go and now I am on my own
Fears and nightmares and fables arise
My friends tell me that I'll be all right
But my friends all have someone and they don't understand
It's not fear of a new one but the one from the start
Did I make a mistake and lose all I had?
Or is it okay that I was left behind?

Walking Away from Love

The wind chill reached a maximum
The words seized in the puff midair

Punching words was a talent
Attraction to the pair

The sudden change of electricity
Emotion drowning hearts minute by minute

Mile by mile when backs saluted
Sudden change of tracks

Pulling and tugging at the guts
Hand over hand yards at a time

Puking empty coughs
Punching empty stomachs

Can't rid of the feeling of empty
Can't change loving him

Answers to Defend

The seasons have passed me by
Terrorizing and agonizing my life
The wind the cool the heat such change
Has destructed every bit of the dream
The dream we built and the future of it

I can't remember what life was like with you
A trance
Easy to say that somebody else will take your place
To recreate to restore to repair
My sudden change of a path

I ask myself why I let you go
No answer in razor blades
Nor in selling my body in excess
Will a sugar pill ever do the trick
Will my voice ever be heard

I let you go with no answers to defend

I sit and wonder if my life will define whom I have loved
The seasons erased my beautiful sculptures
Who will know of such contact
Trust Work
Time spent Feelings shared
My face disappears in the horizon

It's hard to say whether life has a better plan
It's harder to figure out what to do with this broken heart

The seasons came and claimed themselves on my emotions
The spring the summer the fall

I don't know if I'll make it through another one
The winter holds the key to my happiness
Ironic in a plethora of levels

Lonely Road

I could pay attention to the road.
After all, I am behind the wheel.
But I rather not.
Not a big loss after all. If anything...
Just think I am at the stoplight jamming away my blues
when I look at the car behind me.
Hazy- through the review mirror.
Passenger seat empty; could I occupy such hasty space?
Would that be the ride of my life?
It could, I would in a heartbeat. But what ifs don't work.
I am driving home after work after school after all the juice has
been taken out of me.
I seek to seethe the urge inside me. The blood must boil. Such
passion deploy.
But the road ahead is empty. Filled with pairs to my solo stroll.
I could pay attention to the road.
After all, I am not one to kill.
But I rather let go.
Not a big loss after all.
Since my mind has been lost.
On this lonely road.

Jingle Keys No More

Driving is not as fun anymore
Every day the chances of driving off a cliff increase
My mind is not okay to take me to work
Unfortunate that my license can't restrict a broken heart
Stamp away right next to organ donor and let the police know
that the reason I cut those cars off and my slight speeding up
are all because of love
Blame it—Dare to
Love has imposed itself on my driving abilities
It's made my sight a complete haze
And all my ears can hear is the melancholic melody exuding
from the speakers
A fast-paced suicidal vehicle roaming the streets
I should not be the only passenger
The bus- yes- the bus is the way to go
Plenty of witnesses to testify and explain to the judges of how
love terminated my life
Instantaneous
So I will place my car keys next to the remote control on top
of my night stand
My license locked away for good
Or until my arms stop shivering in the humid summer days
I stroll instead
Across the street toward the park or any place that will be able
to take me
The person in the car speeding my way doesn't know
That irony will rue this day
My keys never to jingle in my hands
Love- victoriously took me down

Must Your Face Go with It?

Losing you torn me apart, losing you and all we had
has to be the toughest thing life has thrown in my direction.
But all the pieces have fallen into place now that we are apart.
Don't get me wrong; I still love you.
Yet it's different.
New.
Out with the old.
Ha, it tickles me since I've heard I would never love at all or
enough.
Again, like I did with you.
I disagree.
Life can always go up. Only, go up.
Yes, I've come to know that life holds no guarantees.
Optimism is the way I choose to live my life.
Since you left my side, I have gone through the motions.
Life tried its best to break me into pieces.
Everything crumbled once you set your sight over the
horizon.
Hardened you have made me.
Not that it was necessary.
Either way, I am happy.
New goals and new territories are what I am after.
Something you could not nor wanted to offer me.
When I look back then forward
I realize you were a delayed rest.
Not saying you were a mistake.
All the words said were meant and as you know
I don't use regrets.
But I keep on walking to my destination.
Direction
you lack.
You have gone back where you came from.

I salute you.
And hope for the best.
Through it all, I tried my best to make my wish come true.
To keep you close
and
erase all signs of struggle off our faces.
Since, I have been thrown into a bucket.
The calls unreturned.
Emotion lifeless without any emphasis.
Still I look at you quite fondly.
Hoping that fate was correctly misplacing us together.
Now, I am dancing away,
energized and passionate.
I am still spastic and strong-minded but maybe
I can be handled like I did with your persona.
A balance, that most times, we failed to achieve.
I run through my days smiling
and hoping the tiny opening of depression
and self-mutilation you left me with will for once
disappear.
And if your face must go with it, so be it.

Wishing You Well

The pictures with you in them lay on the floor
This keeps me from ripping away those memories
It's tough I'd say as the days blend together
The funny thing is I miss you more and more each of those
troubled days
I scratched the wall
My desk will never be smooth again
The carpet shows signs of tear from that split second
I have been crawling for hours...
I can't wake the entire house
I cry I howl all within the power of my strength to keep it all
inside
Couples are innocent—friends are absent
Since best bud was an attribute you took with you
I just saw the first picture of you with him
I have to say you pick us well
He's attractive but can he make you feel the way the
predecessor did?
Does he?
Does he taste better than I? Does he last all night?
Can he?
Holding his hand and hugging his spine
Does it tingle your insides?
Do you sleep at night dreaming of the days that will be?
The big grand house you wanted in the south?
Does your dream become a reality?
Your parents' approval and your silly wedding bliss?
I hope you achieve that and more
That's why I sit here I ponder the idea of a whore
Goes well with my well-spread reputation
Do you believe that? Of course you do- you don't know me
anymore

I do- remember you- all of it
From your silly laughs and your loving words
The cd you made me and my loving notes
I helped you- you made me
Such bliss is all here! You knew that- what happened?
You loved me- I remember
I still remember...
I can feel it I now need it and though the end was rough I love
you so
Do you sleep at night? Have you ever thought of me?
I agree- there's no need.
When you loved someone that you were going to marry
It's the fair game of love you play
Well done
I wish you well...

Happy for Your Move

Hung up the phone on your voice
A tone of content
I sit back with a tear rolling down
You have what you were dreaming of
The opposite of who I was
With you

You're moving
Back to happy
Like you wanted
Without me

I let go of our love
And you found what you were looking for

I'm happy
I truly am
I love to see you smile

I wish I were the reason
But I'm happy for you

Regardless it pains me strangely
That you are moving on
Moving in with the one

The one that took my face away
Like you wanted soothing the pain
Dreams are made of content

Like your voice
Hanging on the line

I cry out loud
Too *happy* to oblige

Validate Doubt

Celebrated another first month
Now you're moving out together

How am I supposed to feel
Know I spoke the words of our demise
We ended on a bitter November
But I have tried *standby*

Love to hear your voice
Have thought about holding you close
Almost do when you stop by
But I find myself alone

In your presence
In your absence

Validated my choice
Hesitated such luck
Envied your steps
Confused more day by day
Emotions of yesterday trap me
Remember our first

Why is it so important for me to hear you say so
Do you remember
Does it matter if it's past
Can I ever get you back

A part
The whole
I love you
Do you

It's hard for me to know
That you hold him like I was once held
That you kiss him with those lips that caressed mine
It pains me in the gut that he took my place
He's done a better job
Keeping you happy

Doubt myself nowadays
In regards to what I can offer

Ring of Reign

The ring fell on the mattress;
the place where we don't go.
The bond went with our passion.

Blame is on me because I read the signs.
Reasoning behind giving it another try.

I miss my ring.
With it, my virginity left
and my hopes of a one and only.
I can't be first again.
Engaged.

The bolt and chain.
I miss my ring of reign.

Love and Hate

I haven't looked after our star
Maybe when memory fades
love goes with it
I'm ashamed to recognize
that I let you go
A love so strong
Honestly at this point
couldn't tell you
If I want to be with you or not
I miss you I love you
You know that
It pains me that we are so far apart
Memories of kids
Nobody like you
My dream I confess
still lies in you
I HATE the fact that now I have to say
like you no one else
will I LOVE the same again

No Longer You

I need the moist freeze on my forehead
like a cloth in the summertime
Or at dawn when a virus
Holds me as its prey unexpected
A set of hands to rub my back
My stomach my arms
Toes tingle with sensations
Love was able to get me through the days
Through anything
Protecting me with a robe
A bubble blocking away the *pests*
I remember then
The missing ingredient
The image of
The thought of
The fact that there is no longer you

We Got Each Other

We truly understood
Now bodies parted
The rest withdrew
Psychology tries to
But doesn't explain
The reasons behind
You walking away
I broke your heart
Inflicted the pain
You took my life
Now there's nothing left
For me to enjoy
For me to look for
There's nothing in me
I'm crawling alone
Dreams stars
The tears in my eyes
I have lost you both
My friend and my guy
Your friendship your love
I'm willing to die

Other fool
Two men making a whole
completeness—achieved
One kiss one hug
Entire world could only wish
Sincerity—a gift
Only thing standing in the way is me being selfish and cruel
You happy again with some other fool

Tears Not Dry

The streets are tainted
my pleasures drown the pavement
Pairs of eyes enticed by
such powerful resentment
I have been hated but never like this
not since I have been easy to hit
Target I have become
with the strength of my red veil
Eyes have become teary
circles reign my stance
As walkers pass me by
sniffing the lonely
Craving the tactless
to imprint fingertips
Over my canvas
to use me to spare me
Not wanted just left with
a mark across my chest
My forehead letting others know
of my misfortune
Let them attack again
my mind uneasy
My tears not dry
pedestrians walk around
The pavement still hot

Truly & Forever

I want to break my head open
I have tried
On the wall, on the night stand, on the door
This feeling reminds me of Enis
Yet mine feels far worse

The empty space in me is the same
But you are not dead
Unfortunately
Reminding me daily of whom I miss

You forgot of me
Or are you going to tell me you were going to call
If I happen to do so after weeks of no talk

You don't love me anymore
That is a big difference
I was not made your star
With love and desire
With compassion nor a tie

I am punching the words out of my mouth
The cries are howls within my room
I don't have you- nor a friend
So I have been by myself
A big mess listening to repeats of *Sugababes*

It's true- they are right
I can't cope with your smile
Your face- any longer
There's a hole in my heart that will make it stop soon
So I sit and cry and I think of you
'Til I'm done and I die I will be forever yours

I Want You Back

Cannot be uttered to you
I might have lost my mind
With letting you go
But I left behind the thoughts of suicide
A long time ago

It pains me in the groin
The fact that the world knew
It knew this would happen

Fate history or some other bullshit
It jinxed with heartache
We were not supposed to last
But why did we begin?

The anguish of the days has left me with no gift
Like you were to me
You saved me from misfortune from drifting
Almost drifted in the discolored blues
But you saved me

I know what happened
I know I'm twisted
The hourglass had done its part
Hearsay was waiting to claim victory

I spoke wise words
With them I left myself alone

You made me aware of the power of my words
I can't imagine you crying through your days
Not seeing through the haze

That emptiness creates from the moment we were over
To the moment you confessed
You had found the one to help
You transgress from the pain
To emptiness
From my words to better days
Are you willing to convince me?
Convince me of the transverse?
I can't seem to imagine that was the case
Specially since my tears get in the way
This is the persona I was left with
From our end

I wish you could convince me of my worth
That would elongate my stay on earth
Before demise finds a way
Pissed doesn't explain how I feel
Thinking of the world against me
Against the things I hold dear
You and I are over with
My life holds no candle to the goodness
The goodness that we had

Now I'm struggling to keep afloat
On top of the drowning of this world
Disillusioned by insincerity
By the pollution of the heart
The fact that you don't remember who we are
Forgetting me and who I am
Has to be the worse than dying alone
Since my imprint washed off the surface
Of who you are Of such love

I stand on solid ground
The one to break me apart

All the insecurities I keep still
They won't change
I feel like I have lost you
For good that's a fact

No matter how much I wish it were true
For my sanity
I won't utter I want you backs

This World Won't End

Skies black with envy
Eyes parted from the subject
Judgment
Passed again and again
Rules of being lonely
The world can't make the person
But a person can't make it alone
Clouds roaming have become friends
Silent
Away from the talking heads
Such world that has stuck a knife
With such strength
Remains
Untamed by the walks of life
If colors are not to smile
And words are not to last
The faces to pass
And the pain to linger at last
Then black skies will color the days
The lovers will stay acquaintances
The winter the summer will remain trends
Depression will rule and such world won't end

I felt you breathe
On me
Beside me
Spooning has never been so subtle
You had me I had you
Ecstasy
The morning light shone bright
Will you be mine forever?
I wonder...

Excuses Are Mine

Reach out to you
To own you
Wish to tangle you in a web
An excuse A test
I could if I wanted
The devil in me
To have you To hold you

Let's make love

Then I can posses you
By the inches of your skin
By the endings of your nerves
Tug you in a twist
By the realization of your confusion

Touch me Kiss me
Make me yours again
Be mine to spare
To cherish To shelf

Devil is I
Excuses are his
Intentions strong and solid
My feelings don't exist

-CONFUSION-
STOP!!!

I'm on the floor gasping for air
You are on a bed full of quick breaths
Make love to him

While I fight with myself

A chain around my neck
His hand steady on mine
The Devil is near
I weep I'm terrorized

I need help
You are the first one on my mind

Unbalanced / Lonely

There was a higher power
Not mighty
Clothes came off bodies
With a sweat caressing curves of skin
There is nothing to blame
But a weakness remains
How to rid of such instincts
Of animal carnality
Not trying to find loopholes
Yet loneliness can reach a maximum
Too much of lacking
Can lead to overexposure
Experience earned
Skin cold in the bright light
Unseen
Now naked
Pure
Now tainted
Lack of love can make this happen

Guilt Trip

Tired
Gods inscribed my future before
Can't escape
There is such a baggage
Bullshit
I can only see with my eyes
If carnality is what inspires passion
Am I to blame
Can you blame me
Nonsense
I've lived through the years
Trying to locate such place in my soul
But I can't anymore
I want to be able to see that love is staring back at me
I want such treasures
Presented to me
As if the packaging was undeniably necessary to function
Touch hold and retain such physical beauty
My eyes need love sometimes
I'm tired to oblige
No
No more
I shall return to facilitate
To a raw organic plane
Of ugly and noticeable beauty
Not confusing the two of them
If what my mind creates comes true
Then I will get a God to please
Me
Reestablish carnality
Such human being in me
Animalistic Instincts

The wrong place to label those feelings
There will be no guilt trip
For achieving a dream

Rebuttal

My obsession with pornography
My obsession with my anatomy
Will it ever stop? Haven't I had enough?
I will be so sore. Again.

How lonely can a person be?
The bad news is that I own the answer
There is no solace in my sleep
I keep on giving into my fears. Again.

No, not of being an amateur
But of being so cold, alone. Again.

This closeness is not me
Why do I carry this fantasy on?
It's not me in what I see
But I'm enticed by my palm. Again.

There's nothing wrong with me
Since the majority could be found guilty
But there's a problem with my dream
Sight intact, but there is no vision
                    no vision of this dream.

A Dream

To be forever as one

One heart, one mind, one body

I need to feel the embrace as my skin is under guard

Protected

For no one else to touch, to bruise

Since I've been walked on before

Is it a waste of time to worry?

Time- The trickiest of them all

I must hold on somehow—Someway to this dream

To retain my sanity—So my heart can blossom

There's hope in me still, of that perfect match

No longer alone hoping to watch

Others be happy and not me

Is it wrong for me to seek

In the worst of places?

Is it wrong for me to hold on to my dream?

House Arrest

I wish I could keep myself from wanting you
I rather rip my heart into shreds than be with you
I know what I am getting myself into
But I can't keep myself from wanting you

I wish I could look the other way whenever you come near me
Since you will only play with my mind
I am aware of masochism
But I can't handle your power over me

You disgust me and I want you
Only bring anguish but I can love you
I'm open to you and you better know how to handle me
Because you will know what fear truly means

I wish I could control my urges
But I rather play along
I wish I could stop the desire
But your kisses I long

I wish you knew the truth behind my face
I wish you the best of luck
I wish you knew the truth behind this name
I rather love you but I'm okay with house arrest

Spectrum

So you had me for a night
What's the verdict
Am I a used cow
Now I ponder why
And if I should have kept
Not my pride but to myself
But you wouldn't be impressed

Why am I thinking of you

I should keep my hands in the air
Remaining tucked
Not plump for you to see
Yet wishing is unable to turn back time
With its hands ticking away
At my hopping and wishing
And stopping the thinking...
I know what I did
With no regrets
But could I have salvaged a tiny spectrum of myself

Passion Frowns

Enter me
Through my skin
Gaps of eagerness willingly

Irony is bedding me
Since nobody else will

Irony is bedding me
Because that is what I allow
Fears of loneliness
Make my passion frown
Detached from emotions
Balance of it all is beyond my comprehension

Control me
Through my extremities
Length expressing bluntly

Empty air is my bedmate
A person too heavy to be compacted in the hasty space

Empty air starts to creep in
Inside a person not easy to live with
Understanding the heights of my expectations
Allowing doubt to name the days ahead
Fear from loneliness
My passion non-existing
Enter me through my skin
Control me through my extremities
Allow me to occupy my bed fully
Help me express my love bluntly

Philadelphia

Driving to Philadelphia
One of my proudest moments
The car drove itself
He as my guide As my map
He took care of me

I kissed a giant
Conquered a fear
Of loathsome proportions
I began to love my presence again

Urged the night to kill me
Have played by awful rules
Kept my enemies very close

The dark could not find me
But it taunted me
A building
Thirteen stories high
Did look out the window

The cold pavement
Could have been pushed
In my deep sleep taken
With one eye opened
Visuals of dark flesh and loathsome lies

But I tamed the giant
With a kiss I was saved
From myself
Over confident

I drove away in the falling skies
White was all I could see
The giant left behind
Playing by itself

No dust on the frozen pavement
My heart in an empty box
My mind up my sleeves
Left a dark room with one big blue ball
My eyes on the prize
Such a giant defeat

Packing what I have left
Should not be time consuming
I put my hefty baggage on
My back and start
The balancing act

I take this bag to my destination-

That's All

I miss you baby. Haven't heard your voice.
I miss you baby (that's all).

Haven't been lucky since (you).
I pray that someone else (soon)
is out there, like you, that's all I care.

My Phone is always on nearby;
I guess, my head doesn't want to understand
that it's over, I just miss you, that's all.
Accustomed to you, and your touch.
How were we wrong? That I don't know.
I followed my heart, that's all I can tell you.
The day reminds me of you every chance it gets.
Don't seem to *move on* through each breath I take.
I even dreamt of making sweet music together.
I don't know now, though one can never say never.

I wanted you here and you gave me *the drift.*
Don't want to live like this, but that's how life is.

I hear your name everywhere (and)
I see your face everywhere!
And every time I try to hide, I see you even there!
It's not fun but I miss you.
It's not right but I do.
You weren't the one for me but I need you tonight.
I need a friend to hold my hand.
To hear your Jokes, can never have enough of you, my baby.
To feel your touch, to have you near.
To feel your company, that's all I need.

Haven't been lucky since (you).
I pray that someone else (soon)
is out there, unlike you, that's all I care...

I miss you baby, no one else I need.
I miss you baby with every inch of me.
I miss you baby. Haven't heard your voice.
I miss *you* baby (that's all).

That I Hope

Although the decision was Right
and we have to *move on*
You will stay with me forevermore
you gave me a taste of what I want
You gave me a light with your smile
That I hope you know
You made an impression
I will never forget you
I enjoyed our strong connection
You sure made an impression
I will never forget you
Short-lived but everlasting
Circumstances made it hard for me
I wasn't in it to Play, I truly cared
About you and your feelings
Did not mean harm
I cried myself to sleep that night
I cried by myself after that call
I truly cared
Differences made us blend
Our humor, the Jokes, a match in heaven
No one like you before
That I hope you know
You changed my future
The ruler in which everyone will be measured with
Your lips, your hands
Your touch, your smell
In the atmosphere they still remain
Wasn't in it to play, I truly cared
That I hope you know
You made an impression

I will never forget you...
And that I hope you know.

wink-wink at me again

Chiseled by Parts

There was a natural embrace
One big pile of wanted love
It's hard to duplicate
Specially because time keeps passing by
Though the power of the positive is untamed
The time does take away
Bit by parts
To emphasize the frailty of things
My head held high
Chiseled in its form
Lonely in its stance
Without an ounce of love
There was a chemical embrace
Done trying to replicate
I miss it I want it
But I will have it again
Chiseled in my form
Tough in my stance
I pray that I keep holding on
Being in love and keeping my word

Compare and Contrast

Keeping the picture of your face above me always
Photographs are tricksters
Only show what is missing now
Your love
I will keep you in my heart
Not letting go of the past
If you and I are not to be as one
Then I'll take you to the next
To compare and contrast

At Once

One is at a zip code's reach
once the ink is splurged
on a white-lined dove
Another is a call away
from DC to LA
the kisses of fire
that tangle me in a web
Le garcon mignon
the best of encouraging mistakes
of a friend's leftovers
I have plenty to choose from

I've never been in love so much

Le Tour Eiffel

Tommy can't wait to get on a plane
To rush back home
For Ryan—To him
To wrap his arms around him
Laying his lips softly against the wind of opportunity
The feeling unlike anything he felt before
Sure this affair had not evolved as much as he wanted it to
But Paris made the decision
He flew miles away from his heart's desire
He's been waiting to realize
Hoping to realize that patience is indeed a virtue
He won't be disappointed
Diving into new and better opportunities is not hard to do
Not for Tommy
Not for Ryan
Not even for love
Though time can have its impact on an uncertain future
Its hands can tick toward any direction
So the flight awaits itself
Tommy still miles away nowhere near an aircraft
Ryan waits awake at night
Hoping that Tommy feels the same

Content

Who can blame me

If you are so edible

Yes you're tainted

With unwritten rules

A friend's X

Am I violating a code

Who the hell cares

I love you so much

You brought joy into my life

From Paris to my heart

Tres Bien

Et content

From your eyes to your lips

I cannot wait for your trip to end

So we

Together

Can embrace

those feelings we had

From the night that we met

I see you with me and it's eerie to say

That I can see my being as part of a set

With you

Tres Bien

Et content

You brought the passion

and humid we get

With steam

In a car

With the sweetest of dates

And the greatest of nights

The passion it flourished

in the blink of an eye

You became a trend

A savior of my end

A demise so premature

you were able to save

Me

As of now

I'm a hundred percent

More efficient with love

Such ideas in my head

Tres Bien

Et Toi?

Kisses and Angels

The best date twice in a row
You really have staying power
Within me—beneath me

I have been thinking about your embrace.
Ever since we met two years ago.
Briefly, I had it, but it was let go for reasons we both are aware
of.

Patience has been more than a virtue. And more of a gift.
Your body trembles just enough every time I come nearby.

Your kisses, oh so gentle, can do that all night long.
Your place is quite accommodating; I can see myself crashing
on your bed
next to you, sharing eternity.
The skin of your hands blends perfectly with mine with
addition to the
perspiration we both exude when our bodies get too hot to
handle.

I will forever be okay with letting you hold me as we both look
into the horizon,
through such tinted windows in such cozy of a life.
Why did it take us this long?

You'd think I care. The truth is, I am beyond discovering the
way God works.
Mysteriously attaching healthy obstacles on each individual
angel I have encountered.
Learning I do. And Loving, I allow.
Your kisses, oh so gentle, can captivate me all night long.

Take It or Leave Me

Night has grabbed a hold of me just as you have.
Again.
Emotionally avoiding sleep in order to facilitate my train of
thought.
One word from your mouth—not even.
The idea of you being around somewhere near absorbed me.
I want to become a pro at stalking.
Stalking your every move.
I need to know you
smell you—breathe you- hold you
see you, spy on you as a hawk in the night sky.
Feeling the presence of its prey.
Wondering around waiting to attack.
Crazy you've made me.
The world wants this of me.
It's two am and I am lying down
on a hard-surfaced, unoccupied bed.
Thinking and roaming.
Getting ready for the heist.
(I love you -whispers-)
We have known each other for a while,
long years in our lifestyle.
You want me, I want you.
Now is the perfect time for us.
But one day of bliss here
and one day of bliss there
cannot compare to a lifetime of love.
Is it enough?
What is? What does?
If you could explain to me what is and what isn't.
Don't feel I have the time to waste playing games.
Weeks become days

in my crowded-manic head.
We sealed a silent pact.
With our lips and unspoken words.
Feelings.
Maybe I have gotten used to saying such things.
Why would the reason matter?
I could bake a pie -or-
order Chinese food
-or- pizza with mushrooms.
I could take you on a picnic -or-
to your favorite restaurant
-or- make an announcement
whilst a get together.
Most likely just the two of us
watching the sunset in such a perfectly placed balcony;
for the world to see.
Happiness now completed.
I want you, you want me.
It is the perfect time for us.
To celebrate this gift God and his helpers
have worked so hard on.
It finally happened
And all I ever want to do is...
(Love you -whispers-)
Is it too early to say?
Will it make a difference?
Damn it—I love you!
Take it or leave it.
I won't waste time playing games.
Love me or leave me.

BOY

I feel like a little boy again
Roaming the streets
Cruising to see what there is for me to grasp
Obtain with virgin eyes and an open mind

I did my time
I still do
Did more than a few

Experiences
But feel like starting again
After love left a stain

I recharge and go back out there
I feel like a child
My mind is clear again

A fresh start
The aura is not overtaken

I have control
I make the decision
I make the call
I am a boy again

A Light in My Head

By turning a light in my head
You make me explore the uncertain
Raindrops too familiar
Colorful shades of loneliness
Could I ever be happier?
With a thought, you could guess
But reality settles
And the pain sharply remains
Alone is a way of being yet loneliness is a habit that stays

Smiles Help Pretend

A smile can be consuming
An idea so promising
Two people in too many situations
The eyes play a part
Sparks—
But life is present
Ideals run out the back door
A far away dream
You could be the perfect bride
I'd embark in such journey
But a smile only helps me pretend
And phallic art hovers my name

If Only You Knew

You pour your eyes all over me.
I'm drenched in a liquid of longing amid blushing.
There is something about you.
I've been here to notice.
Every other day you invest yourself in me.
I have to admit, there's a strong curiosity.
I wonder what you can do for me.
Your lips so subtle and your eyes ever so sparkling.
There is something about you.

(Something about this girl.)

You make me ponder whether I can be another being—
Another being with you.

All these ideas roam in my head
as fast as my brain can follow.
Then the professor dismisses our class.
The dreams of you and I
destroyed by the power of time.

The truth is, that is not where the line is drawn.
I will coyly step out the doors
where my destiny is waiting.
An arm around my neck
and a kiss on both my cheeks.
His fingers will caress mine
and my curiosity with be far diminished.

You Can Advise Me

There are skid marks on such face
Remains of a smile flaccid and stretched
If you see right through tears and laughs
You are able to feel a slight vibration
To see a flame
Colors explode
Lighting the cynicism toward the dark
Toward a safe home
Lock away
Feelings of pain and remorse
I love you
I dare you to love me back

Wise words are spoken
But it is easier to be the advisor
And not the recipient

Part of Me

Gullible??
Proudly.
Waiting for the day to end.
To run to my secret vault
and throw those books back on my bed.
Mathematics can't teach you how to love.
Only emphasizes the trouble of your tries.
Pronunciation doesn't work,
in such languages,
many ways to say one love.
So I forget what I've learned;
And I venture into life to learn from myself.
To throw myself in situations that may hurt me in the end.
But this is how to learn.
Yet I don't think of such things.
The excitement sips into my skin.
Tantalizing my every nerve
in order to see such happy thoughts.
Reflecting in my eyes.
With pixels to spare with
my every idea
my every dream.
Yes, this may not be real.
But can you explain reality to me again?
This may not last.
But I'm waiting and I am running
away from troubled minds.
I'm sitting in a throne.
The decisions, always mine.
Can't wait to look into your eyes.
I'm living day by day.
Meaning, you are already a part of my life.

Pixels

Showing in a tiny frame
Only pixels to obtain
It's a pretty sight
Color after color for my eyes
But will it transcend
Is there a being in those shots
A hand to hold
Perhaps
A kiss could not reach around the cables and gigabytes
And the plastics and such space within time
But I believe
Emphasize
Is such thought that gives a life
Optimism
To close one's eyes by the turn of the darkened night
So flashes come this way
And colorful frames I obtain
Remembering nothing is what it seems
But that dreams still do exist

Space in Time

A date in cyberspace
The best kind
End at the click of a mouse
But no interruptions
No unhappy thoughts
You and I will get together
Eliminating any structure in between
That may interfere with
The connection that already exists
I love you
Since there is love for the idea
Such idea becomes you
And two can become one
Two in a million of surfing minds
And with heavy serendipity
You and I
Managed to combine interest
With laughs
—blooming hearts
Tingle in hands
I want you to be mine
but love will run its course
and Picture frames
Speed of light
Will forever be the reasons why

We are lucky
To have this—
Precious moment in time

Bobby Maguee

Our lips met
possible by my willingness.
The bed was over-crowded
but you and I found privacy.
We truly met this humid night.
Previously lacked the weight of conversation—
frugal with meaning.
Tonight we were introduced.
Through spinning bottles—
flashes blinding the curiosity—
friends laughing their energy away…
On a chilly night we met.

Kissing you was instinct—
impulsed by perfect fingertips.
Fueling the energy capacity,
you became alive in front of my wondering eyes.
There is still enough mystery.
Every characteristic as Bobby Maguee.
Kiss me more.
Hug me again—emphasis in meaning.
Wanting limitless sessions—
true facts of needing.

Thank you for coming tonight.
I needed a savior.

It Takes One More

The message read
"I'm free today, would you like to make plans?"
I sighed in relief that my past invitation was not in vain.
Yet I sit at work,
waiting to flee
but I have not answered yet.
Should I begin to be exclusive
not being"the opportunist'?
Why do I feel I have to protect myself?
To love—walls must be walked on.
Cannot cease my tries.
I must keep loving to find the one.
If it takes this one more,
I'll be okay with that.

An Entity

The Light chose me
In this decision I was marked
The power is locked
I know how to reach it
To control it
The Light is within me
I know love—I am love
If I seek—I shall find
Love

Talk to me
He says
Put your trust in me
But I have never seen you
Won't touch you nor feel you
It's hard to believe in something
Not concrete

Then I think
What's the point of life
If your heart's not opened
Open to give hope a try
Believing in love
Believing in one
Another
A soul
A father

So now
I rather
Live alone in a bubble of love
Pretense
Of just
His words
My trust
If that's all it takes to make my heart
Glow
Filling it with dreams
To grow
Than I am up for the challenge

Paint a Color of Serenity

Cleansing cream on my skin
Liberating the pores letting them breathe
The color of serenity
Spread the calm throughout my body

Submerge my mind in the idea of the thought
Detachment
Enlightenment
Love

Violet beams
White streams above my eyes
Underneath my expectations

Will bathe in this miracle
Will let the love creep in

Too

I'm sitting here trying to
figure out why my heart is
full of love
I'm staring at mystery in the eyes
the shape of wants and needs
flaws and needed vice
Full of love
willing and able *too*
I am seeing mystery
in front of the mirror

Pitch Black

Zeus has tried to capture me everywhere I go
I haven't succumbed

The light is present but scarce
The dark is still my knight

I always put myself in awful positions
But I'm holding my ground
Through the shadows
I represent my savior
I've made my world pitch black
In order to walk inside this hole
Inside this snow globe

Comfort as the world lays to rest
I'm the only guardian to attack
Have been petrified as I try not to realize
The streets are not alone and the ground
Has a sound and is not silent
Shadows not imaginative but purely clear

Lamppost flickered
Pinpointed me against the vast lands
Now as I happen to love
The day no longer reigns
Clouds ever so present
Shift the gray through the plains
Allowing Zeus to take a longer rest

He shines in me allowing
Excelling in my heart's mind
Lonely in the night

The days equal to dark
Making my life a dream
Constant ride of cries
I will know that God's son
Guides my way

Symbols are nice on paper

My mind is set
Reach out and there's a hand
Gripping mine
Fast and smoothly

The One Above

I'll begin to spread my wings and fly
Merge between the plains
Get rid of fantasy and aim for an in between
I believe in love
So, why shouldn't I have it?
The boundaries begin to crumble
To disappear
I begin to see my dream
Becoming Clear
All the love I've ever dreamt
It all keeps coming near
Near those accusations of why fatality is not instantaneous
Lingering the pain
If you are not one to be whole
Apart we fall if we don't seem to fit in molds
So I rather dream
Of love and my adventures
I rather dream of love
And deal with the one above

Love Is All That's Needed

There has to be more to life.
Looking for satisfaction is not meant for me.
I have searched but haven't found.
The answer is in the eyes of the world
the world that lacks the strength to overcome.
To stand, alone. To love.
Forgiving all the sins retained in our hearts.
The light above my head
shone away from the horizon
shining the power within.
Helping me see.
The path lies just ahead.
There is a hand holding my stance
along this path.
Scare no more, I see the light.
To change the world, no talent is needed.
To have such luck, is a gift given.

Alone in the Dark

The light came through the blinds as if salvation had chosen
me
I gawked
Mouth opened eyes glued to the spectacle
Rays vibrating past the air surround me
Head to toe
Hugging me tight
Letting me float
Fly around my own body
The wind caressed me
Within the limits of a closed room
A box with a crack
Alone in the dark
Ogled mesmerized
Colors surpassing clarity
More of a vanity
Greatness achieved
The sun smiled at me
Amidst out life-long struggle
I smirked
Allowing the moment to reach me
Inside I knew
What I was doing today
Was my best foot forward
I stood I drank the liquid of tranquility
The light came through the blinds as if for salvation I was
chosen
Rays vibrating past the air surrounding me
Allowing the moment to reach me

Glass Half Full

I didn't give up on the love I found
Music helped my mood
I won't rely on expectations
Just listen to the voice above
Me, consuming, still alone
Not giving up on the love I found

Printed in the United States
200376BV00002B/112/A

9 781424 198580